RADICAL RELATIONS

ROSIE McCORMICK

Belitha Press

First published in the UK in 2002 by

Belitha Press Limited
A member of Chrysalis Books plc
64 Brewery Road, London N7 9NT

Copyright © Belitha Press Limited 2002
Text by Rosie McCormick

Editor: Kate Phelps
Designer: Peter Clayman
Illustrator: Woody
Consultant: Kathleen Robertson

ISBN 1 84138 431 3

British Library Cataloguing in Publication Data for this
book is available from the British Library.

Printed in Italy by Eurolitho S.p.A.

Some of the more unfamiliar words used in this book
are explained in the glossary on pages 46 and 47.

CONTENTS

Dear Reader

I expect that there are times when you go through an entire day, or even days, without thinking too much about some of the people in your life. After all, they're always around doing and saying familiar things. Mum or dad take you to school, they help you with your homework, insist you have a bath and they grumble and groan quite a bit. Brothers and sisters read your comics, mess up your room and borrow your favourite CDs. Your teachers, well they've always got lots to say about all kinds of things. And your friends, well they're just your friends.

So that's that really!

Well, not quite! The fact is, that for large parts of each day, every day, for as long as we are alive, we interact with other people. We form relationships with people. You see we live and experience life with other people. So, how we get along with the people around us affects everything we do. This book is about relationships with family, friends, teachers, even your pet rabbit. It will help you focus some attention on the important people in your life and maybe even help you form some new relationships.

'Can I borrow your bike please'

'No you can't weasel face!'

INTRODUCTION

The incredible thing is that your life will be touched by so many people, too many to count. (Try counting all the people you meet in just one day. You'll be surprised at how many there are – unless you spent the day in bed, of course!) And you yourself will have an effect on other people's lives. In fact you already do because you are someone's child, grandchild, friend, neighbour or pupil. But how do you know how to get along with others?

Usually your parents teach you how to behave in family and other social situations. And, as you experience new things, new people and new situations, you are once again guided by others until eventually you know what is expected of you.

This book will help you relate to the people in your life. Here you will find a guide to good friendships, tips on dealing with bullies, suggestions on how you can help people and much much more. So, read on and discover how you can improve your relationships – and make wonderful new ones.

ALL ABOUT RADICAL RELATIONS

Who are the people who guide you and prepare you for adulthood? Who are the people who love you and protect you? No, it's not a trick question and you shouldn't have to think twice because I'm talking about your family.

FAMILY HABITS

Family groups come in all shapes and sizes. Mums and dads are often married but not always. Sometimes there are lots of brothers and sisters, sometimes just one child. Some children live with either their mum or dad and maybe with step-mums or dads and step-brothers and sisters, as well. Some children are adopted and some are fostered.

The people who care for you and love you are your family.

Why is your brother so small?
He's only my half brother!

GOOD GUIDANCE

Your family, and in particular the adults, not only love you and care about you but they are responsible for you too. That's why they keep a close eye on the things you say and do. And that's also why they spend so much time teaching and guiding you. And, as you approach adulthood,

the many, many lessons on how to behave in the big wide world, the billions of words of advice on how to treat others, will fall into place. You will understand your responsibility towards this planet and the people you share it with.

Your family wants you to be:

Kind and thoughtful
Helpful
Loving
Generous
Happy
Honest

Your turn!

You have an important role to play, not just as someone who is learning about life but as a helper or teacher. By helping and playing with younger brothers, sisters or even cousins, you are teaching them the things you know. Remember that you need to set a good example because they will almost certainly copy you. You can teach them how to paint, draw, play with sand and water, lay the table, wash their hands and get dressed. You can read to them and play fun games with them too. To them you are very important, you are older and wiser and can do lots of things they can't. You are their special big brother or sister.

Friends

Friends play a big part in your life as well. Having good friends is magical, wonderful and enormous fun. You share so many things – most importantly your childhood. But even the strongest friendships can have ups and downs. As you get older, you will begin to expect more from your friends, and they will expect more from you. This is what makes friendship more complicated. Trust and loyalty become important issues, especially when it comes to keeping and not breaking promises. So a little thought and a bit of effort can make all the difference when it comes to being good friends.

The Guide to Good Friendships

• Friendships last longer and are stronger if you care about how your friends feel.

• Congratulate your friends when they do well and thank them when they do things for you.

• If a friend is feeling sad or lonely, try to comfort them. Try to think of things that might cheer them up, or simply listen if they need to talk.

'Just co-operate with me!'

Mum: 'Ben, if you don't turn that music off I will go mad!'
Ben: 'Too late mum, I turned it off an hour ago'.

• One of the most important friendship guidelines is to put yourself in 'your friend's shoes'. This simply means that when there's a problem, you need to think about things from your friend's point of view, not just your own. This is one of the best ways to solve problems. It's important to remember that not everyone sees things the way you do.

• Never boss, bully or exclude others.

• Being too competitive can spoil things. It can turn a fun game into a contest with winners and losers. Doing things with your friends is about having fun not who is best.

• The best way to make a good friend is to simply be one.

• You can't have too many friends.

TEACHERS ARE FRIENDS TOO

Teachers, yes I did say teachers, play an incredibly important role in your life. They are friends but they also have a very special job to do. They will spend years struggling to get you to understand or remember all kinds of things. They are preparing you for adulthood by developing your skills and talents. So, in order to teach you and help you to learn as much as possible, teachers need your respect and a little bit of effort. The more you put in to your school days the more you will benefit from them. Believe it or not, when you are all grown up, you will remember many of your teachers and the effect they had upon your life. They are some of the best friends you will ever have.

ANIMAL FRIENDS

Having a pet is great fun but it's also a big responsibility. It's almost the same kind of responsibility that you have towards your friends. Your pet will rely on you not to let it down. It will need your time and attention, your care and your love. If you feel that your life is too busy then don't get a pet that you can't care for. Wait until you have enough time in your life to care for a furry, feathery or scaly friend. And like all friendships, you will discover that your pet friend will most certainly care for you too.

10

DETECTIVE WORK

Not all our views and beliefs come from our families and friends. More and more we are influenced by newspapers, magazines, advertising, TV and music.
It's important to stop and think about the things you read, hear, see and listen to. Ask questions about this constant flow of information. Think about whether you agree with the articles and stories in newspapers and magazines. Check other sources of information, such as the Internet, or talk to adults to make sure you are getting the facts. Examine the language being used. Does it sound like it is trying to make you feel or think a certain way? Don't be influenced by advertising. Make sure you want the product not the packaging. Remember, sometimes you have to do a little detective work to get to the truth!

BULLYING

Now when it comes to dealing with people, there is one thing you must never, ever do and that is to bully someone else. It is unkind, cruel and harmful. So don't do it! Got that? Bullying includes calling people names, making things up to get someone into trouble, hitting, pinching, biting, pushing and shoving. It also includes taking things away from someone, damaging their belongings, stealing their money and taking their friends away too. Bullying is so bad that it can make someone become too frightened to go to school.

LET SOMEONE KNOW

If you are being bullied, tell a friend, tell a teacher and tell your parents. And tell the bully that he or she must stop – now. It is not acceptable and it is wrong. Bullies are only frightened when people speak up and speak out. It can be hard to do this. Sometimes writing a note to your parents or teacher can help. Or perhaps confide in someone outside the immediate family, like a cousin or grandparent.

ALL ABOUT BULLIES

- They want to feel powerful.
- They are prepared to hurt other people to get what they want.
- They feel hurt inside.
- They find it difficult to see things from someone else's point of view.

What do you call an angry giant?
SIR!

Wise up

It's important to understand that people with special needs or disabilities aren't different, they are just like you. They are only different in the way you are from your friends. One of your friends may be tall with blonde hair, another may be short with dark hair and you may be of medium height with red hair. People with special needs or disabilities don't see things differently, don't feel things differently and they sure don't want to be treated differently. Okay!

WHAT HAPPENS
IN YOUR NEIGHBOURHOOD

Not everyone is as fortunate as you but you may not have noticed. For example, there are children who would love to have just one or two of the dozens of toys you have stacked in your bedroom. There are others who would love to belong to the kind of family you have. And there are elderly people who live alone and may not talk to or see anyone for days. These people are your neighbours; you share the same community. How about giving them some time and attention too?

TAKE ACTION NOW

• Elderly people who live alone can feel isolated. There is so much you can do to make their day brighter.

• With adult supervision, visit elderly people who live alone.

• Help elderly neighbours with their gardening or offer to go to the library or shop for them.

• Offer to walk an elderly person's dog or help care for their cat.

When do you know when a dog is fully mature? After they have their Bark-mitzvah!

14

A HELPING HAND

Children everywhere love to play with toys or wear a new outfit or have a special treat. Just imagine if you didn't have any of these things. Well there are children, probably not too far away from where you live, who hardly ever get any of these things. Their families don't have enough money to pay for them. I can tell already that you would love to help them.

A good way to begin is to get your class and school involved in raising money for some charities. You can also encourage everyone you know to donate toys, clothes, all kinds of things, to charity shops and churches. You and your friends could think of new kinds of wacky fundraisers.

Sponsored Baked Bean Bath Sitting

Friends that need help

All over the world there are children, just like you. But some of them do not have enough food to eat, do not have a school to go to and some have to work all day long to help their families to survive.

You may think that there's nothing you can do to change things. After all you don't know them and they are too far away for you to help them. But you are affected by these people and their lives all the time. Just look at the variety of food items in your local supermarket or the range of products in a large department store. The food you eat, the clothes you wear, even the furniture and electronic equipment in your house may have been made in poorer countries by poor people. It's okay to buy these things because when richer countries trade with poorer countries, they help to fight poverty. However, it's important that we all make sure that the people who grow or make these products are treated fairly and not exploited.

A watchful eye

This is where you come in. More and more people around the world are demanding that the things they buy have been produced without exploitation – that is, that the farmers or factory workers who grew the food or made the products received a fair price for their work and that their working conditions are clean and safe.

You can encourage all your friends and their families to buy goods that are known to have been made according to fair-trading guidelines. Often packaging will give you this information, or you can ask questions at your local supermarket or department store.

Oxfam Fair Trade Company uses this checklist when buying from other countries:
• Workers receive fair wages
• Workers are able to meet to discuss important issues
• Workers are not discriminated against or exploited
• Workers enjoy reasonable working conditions
• Producers take care of the environment

WHAT YOU CAN DO

There are lots of other things you can do to help people far away.

• You can help to raise money for specific charities
• You can shop in charity shops such as Oxfam
• You and your family can sponsor an overseas child's education
• You can donate clothes, toys and all kinds of things to organized fundraisers

It's often best to begin by selecting one action or cause. The time that you put in and the effort you make could help change someone's life for the better.

Food for All

Did you know that 800 million people in the world, many of them children, are malnourished? And two billion people in the world have an unhealthy diet that does not contain enough essential vitamins and minerals so they become weak and ill. Does this mean that there isn't enough food in the world to go round? The answer to this question is NO. In fact the world does produce enough food for everyone but we haven't quite figured out how to share it all out.

What's the Problem?

Part of the problem is the fact that many people in the world can't afford to buy the food they need, even though it is readily available in shops or markets. Unemployment is quite often the reason why. After all, without a job, how do you get money to buy food? In poor countries, some families grow crops on their own small plots of land and have animals. Bad weather conditions that cause drought or flooding, as well as wars, can mean that their food supplies are destroyed. And without money they have no way of feeding themselves. Others have had their land taken away from them but are unable to find jobs that would earn them money.

- You can make other people aware of poverty by putting up posters about the problem.

• You can help fight poverty by buying things from charity shops and jumble sales and by donating your old clothes and toys to charity.

GLOBAL FRIENDS

The key to solving many of these problems is co-operation. You can't on your own solve world hunger or other BIG problems either. But you, your family and your friends working together with millions of other global friends can change all kinds of things for the better. Together you can help to make sure that no one has to feel hungry, scared or alone. You can help to make life fairer and safer. You can fight poverty and injustice. Wow, friends working together can be a powerful force – don't you think?

QUIZ TIME

H ere's a fun quiz to check you've been paying attention!

1 Who are the people who guide you and prepare you for adulthood?
a) Your family
b) Your favourite band
c) Your neighbours

2 What does your family want you to be?
a) Noisy
b) Cheeky
c) Kind and thoughtful

3 Friendships last longer if you:
a) Bribe your friends
b) Imprison your friends
c) Care about how your friends feel

4 What must you never ever do?
a) Walk to school on stilts
b) Bully someone
c) Give your sister's pet rabbit to a friend

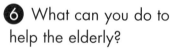

5 What do bullies want?
a) To feel powerful
b) To make friends
c) To play

6 What can you do to help the elderly?
a) Phone them up
b) Nothing, you're too busy
c) With adult supervision, visit them

7 What can you do to help children who do not have all the things you do?
a) Not a lot, you're only a kid
b) Help to raise money for children's charities
c) Write to Father Christmas and ask him to help them

8 It's important to make sure that the people who make or grow things for us are:
a) Treated fairly and not exploited
b) Work hard
c) Start work on time

9 How many people in the world are malnourished?
a) None
b) 1000
c) 800 million

10 Why are people hungry?
a) Some people do not have money to buy food
b) Supermarkets run out of food to sell
c) There aren't enough supermarkets

11 How many people in the world have an unhealthy diet?
a) 20 000
b) 50 000
c) 2 billion

12 Is there enough food in the world to go round?
a) No
b) Yes
c) Maybe

ANSWERS

The China Doll

Megan woke up to the sound of her baby brother crying.
It was still fairly early. The curtains in the room where Megan
slept didn't quite close and she could just about see a dull,
early morning grey-and-pink sky. Sam was crying because he
was hungry, cold and he wanted his nappy changed. Megan
shivered, clutched at her sheet and blanket and pulled her
knees up under her night dress. Then she sighed. There was no
way she was going to get any more sleep.

Megan watched her mum as she changed Sam and poured
some cold milk into a bottle for him to drink. She listened to her
soothing words. They always comforted her as well. Sam
settled down on his mum's lap, gulped his milk and snuggled
as close to her as he possibly could.

Megan, her mum and her brother lived in a special kind of
bed-and-breakfast hotel. They couldn't live at home any more
because Megan's dad had become too scary. He was okay
when he didn't drink. In fact he was kind of nice and played
silly games with her and Sam. But lately he was drunk almost
every day. And when he was drunk he was really mean. He hit
Megan's mum loads of times. The last time he broke her arm
and gave her a really bad black eye. He had also tried to hit
Megan and Sam. That was when her mum had said that they
had to go and live somewhere else. Somewhere far away from
dad. And so they had come to this place.

22

The worst thing was that Megan had to start a new school –
just before Christmas. It was the worst possible time.
She couldn't help thinking about all old her school friends busily
preparing for the nativity play. And then there was the
Christmas Party. She was going to miss out on everything.
Megan tried her best not to dwell on these things but she just
couldn't help it.

'Meggie, you'd better start getting ready for school,' said
Megan's mum. 'Come on, you don't want to be late for the
breakfast club.'

The thought of some warm buttered toast with strawberry jam
and a mug of hot chocolate was enough to make Megan leap
out of bed. Megan grabbed her school uniform from the chair
beside her bed and dashed across the room to huddle in front
of a small electric wall heater. Then she dressed as quickly as
she could.

'Hey madam, don't hog all the heat,' said mum as she
washed and dressed Sam. That done, mum sorted herself out,
put on their coats, strapped Sam into his buggy and they were
ready to go.

It was quite a walk to her new school but Megan didn't mind because on the way there they passed all kinds of interesting shops. Her favourite ones were the flower shop, the bicycle shop, the pet shop and best of all – the toy shop. They always stopped to peer in the toy shop window. Because it was Christmas time, the shop window display was especially impressive. Sam always pointed to a talking Winnie the Pooh and then launched into his favourite song. And as for Megan, well she couldn't take her eyes off a beautiful china doll called Katya. She was Russian and was dressed in a bright red dress, an emerald cape edged with pretend fur and she wore leather lace-up boots. She had the blackest hair and blue eyes. She was the most beautiful thing Megan had ever seen.

Mum had already explained to Megan that Father Christmas wouldn't be visiting them this year but that next year he would make sure that they had a very special Christmas. Megan knew what mum really meant. She could see it etched on her face and hear it in her shaky voice. The fact was their lives were messed up. They didn't have a proper home to live in any more. They didn't have much money so Christmas presents were out of the question. They had to hide from dad and it would probably take ages for things to get better.

All the same, Megan couldn't help wishing and hoping that somehow Katya the china doll would appear, wrapped in sparkling Christmas paper beside her bed on Christmas morning. Oh, and maybe Sam would get his beloved Winnie as well.

In the distance, Megan could see the bright green school gates. Her new school, Chestnut Lane Primary, wasn't too bad. The children in her class seemed alright and her teacher Miss Ross was really nice. One girl in particular, Charlotte Webster, or Charlie to her friends, had made Megan feel really welcome. And a boy called Johnnie Baxter smiled at her a lot. But because Megan didn't want anyone to know about her life and the things that were happening, she hadn't been as nice to them as she should have been.

'Here we are darling,' said mum kissing Megan on the cheek. 'Go inside and get your breakfast. We'll see you this afternoon'

Megan waved and watched as mum and Sam began to make their way back along the busy main road. When they had walked about 50 metres, Megan turned away. She tried not to think about her mum and Sam but it was hard not to. She wondered what they did all day in that smelly, freezing bed-and-breakfast place. Megan shook her head, trying to shake away the thoughts that made her feel so sad. It never worked though, it just made her head hurt.

The dining hall was warm, and it smelled of toast. Megan took her coat off and draped it over the back of a chair. Then she went to the breakfast counter to order her breakfast.

'Toast and jam, please Mrs Riley,' said Megan. 'And can I have a mug of hot chocolate?'

'Coming right up,' said Mrs Riley. 'You go and sit down, luv, and I'll bring it over.'

'Great,' said Megan.

Megan sat down and pulled out her library book. Within minutes her breakfast had arrived. Butter dripped off the edges of her toast and big blobs of strawberry jam covered it.

But she'd hardly read one page of her book and hadn't even finished her first piece of toast when Johnnie Baxter plonked himself down in the seat opposite her.

'Yer don't mind do yer?' said Johnnie with a grin. 'I don't want to sit next to Oscar and Ben anymore. They throw their food around all over the place and I get into trouble,' continued Johnnie. 'If they keep it up, they'll be chucked out.'

'No, it's okay,' said Megan glancing up. 'Sit where you like.'

For a while Megan continued to read her book and munch her toast. She really didn't want to talk to Johnnie. But somehow she knew that Johnnie was staring at her and it made her feel uncomfortable.

Finally, Johnnie broke the silence.

'What yer doin' here anyway. Can't yer mum make yer breakfast?' asked Johnnie.

'It's none of your business,' replied Megan angrily.

'Sorry. I was only asking,' said Johnnie. 'I don't mind telling you why I come here. There are so many kids in our house that my mum can use all the help she can get. So she signed me up for free breakfasts.'

'Oh, really,' replied Megan, trying not to sound too interested. 'How many kids are there?'

'I've got four brothers and three sisters,' said Johnnie between mouthfuls of cornflakes. 'Eight altogether. My old man can't work. He injured his back on a building site. He can hardly walk now. But soon we're gonna get some money because it wasn't his fault. Some bloke wasn't doing his job properly. When the money comes in we're all going to Disneyland. I think I'll get some toast. Do you want anymore?' continued Johnnie, hardly pausing to draw breathe.

'No, I'm okay. Thanks,' said Megan.

Johnnie walked to the breakfast counter and then loaded his plate with buttered toast. Within minutes he was back.

'So yer not gonna tell me huh?' persisted Johnnie. 'There's nothing to be ashamed of. Most people need help from time to time. You're only a kid, you need to eat. That's what my mum says anyway.'

'There's nothing to tell,' said Megan stubbornly.

'Where d'yer live?' asked Johnnie.

'Oh, not too far away,' replied Megan. She was feeling really, really uncomfortable now and she wished Johnnie would go away.

'But where?' said Johnnie.

'Oh, just up the road,' said Megan, as tears began to well in her eyes. She blinked furiously.

IT'S A FACT
Five thousand children a week in Britain suffer a broken home.

Surprisingly Johnnie remained silent for several minutes. Finally he looked up from his plate of toast and stared at Megan.

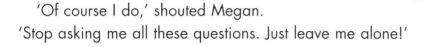

'Don't yer have a home,' he asked softly.

'Of course I do,' shouted Megan. 'Stop asking me all these questions. Just leave me alone!'

And with that Megan grabbed her coat and ran out of the dining hall leaving behind a stunned Johnnie Baxter. When she reached the hallway she burst into tears. She had the most awful, empty feeling inside. It was so scary. It was as if a piece of her was missing. She also felt angry. She couldn't even have a normal conversation with someone anymore. She felt so ashamed about everything and it wasn't even her fault.

Eventually Megan calmed down and made her way towards her classroom. She got there just in time as Miss Ross was just about to close the classroom door. As she walked to her desk, Megan made a point of not looking at Johnnie, and, for his part, he did not look at her either.

Megan loved school, although recently she had been struggling to concentrate. That morning her class were having a spelling quiz. It was such fun that the lesson went really fast and before long it was time for break.

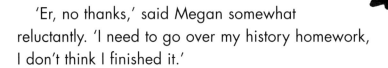

'Would you like to play with me and Kate?' asked Charlie as she and Megan walked out into the bright sunshine. 'We're going to play skipping.'

'Er, no thanks,' said Megan somewhat reluctantly. 'I need to go over my history homework, I don't think I finished it.'

She was lying of course. She had finished her history homework and checked it and even double checked it the night before. But Megan was petrified that Charlie would start asking her loads of questions just like Johnnie had done. Then, when everyone knew about her life, they wouldn't want anything to do with her.

'Maybe tomorrow then?' said Charlie.

'Yeh, tomorrow,' said Megan. And with that she walked off and sat on a wall, pretending to read her history note book.

Moments later, Megan heard a familiar voice.

'I've got another question for you,' said the voice. Megan sighed. She knew it was Johnnie. She didn't reply hoping that if she ignored him he would finally get the message.

'What did the Pacific say to the Atlantic?' said Johnnie.

Megan didn't answer.

'Nothing, it just waved,' continued Johnnie.

IT'S A FACT
More people are now living in poverty than at any other time in the past 20 years.

'Oh and what do you call a donkey with three legs?' said Johnnie again, determined not to give up.
Megan remained silent.

'Wonkey!'
Megan smiled. She didn't want to but she couldn't help herself. Johnnie's jokes were kind of funny.

'See, I knew I could make you laugh,' said Johnnie.

'I didn't laugh, I smiled,' insisted Megan.

'Wow, you're talking to me as well,' said Johnnie as he sat down on the wall beside her.

'What yer doin?' asked Johnnie.

'Just checking my homework,' replied Megan.

'Is that why you didn't want to play with Charlie?' asked Johnnie.

'Yeh,' said Megan simply.

'She's a really nice girl, you know,' said Johnnie. 'When I came here a year ago she and Ben and Oscar made friends with me. They really helped cos things were tough at home. We lost our house when my dad

couldn't pay the mortgage anymore. That was after he got injured. We had to move. We didn't have any money and I had to wear really sad trainers,' said Johnnie.

'In fact I still have to,' laughed Johnnie as he looked down at his feet. 'But any day now we're gonna get some money and then we're gonna go to ...'

'I know, you told me, you're going to go to Disneyland,' interrupted Megan.

'The fact is', continued Megan, 'if you really must know, my family are having a new house built and while we're waiting

for it to be finished we're staying at a hotel,' said Megan, quite surprised by how easily she had made up such a massive lie.

'Oh right,' said Johnnie, clearly unconvinced.

'What yer getting for Christmas?' asked Johnnie, changing the subject so as not to upset Megan anymore.

32

'Oh loads of things, but the main present I think will be a china doll. It's in the toy shop on Eleanor Road. She's beautiful; she's Russian; her name is Katya. My little brother Sam wants a talking Winnie the Pooh', said Megan enthusiastically. 'What are you getting?' Megan asked turning to look at Johnnie.

'Well if the dosh arrives I'm getting a mountain bike. And some new trainers,' laughed Johnnie.

Megan and Johnnie continued to chat about Christmas until the bell rang again. When it did they raced across the playground to line up with their class.

The next two weeks passed very quickly and suddenly it was the last day of school. Megan had kind of made friends with Johnnie and Charlie. She joined in with various games from time to time, but she still avoided their questions and kept herself to herself as much as possible.

Miss Ross had organized a class Christmas party. All the children talked excitedly about Christmas, their presents, what was on TV and, of course, Christmas dinner. Megan joined in, but each time she lied about something it made her feel sick inside.

IT'S A FACT
Two million British children go without at least two things they need (such as three meals a day, toys or adequate clothing).

Three days later it was Christmas morning. To Megan's
surprise, her mum had completely decorated their room with
homemade paper decorations. In the corner was a small tree
with tiny lights and tinsel. And underneath the tree were four
small presents wrapped in red tissue paper and ribbons.

'Wow, mum,' said Megan, 'when did you do all this?'

'While you were sleeping, sleepy head,' laughed mum.
'It's not much really, but I thought it might cheer you up a bit.'

'It's great,' said Megan, jumping out of bed. 'I didn't get
anything for you though mum.'

'I know that,' said mum. 'Come on open up your presents.
You too, Sammy.'

Mum, Megan and Sam sat on the floor together in front of
the Christmas tree. Megan unwrapped the first present. It was

Roald Dahl's *BFG*. She had wanted to read it for ages but it was never in the library. Then she unwrapped the next one. It was a new hairbrush and comb. Megan was surprised and pleased but she still had to force herself not to think about the china doll.

'We'll be having Christmas lunch downstairs at one o'clock,' said Mum. 'So if you like, after you've had some breakfast, we can go for a long play in the park.'

Megan and Sam had great fun in the park. For a while they had the play area all to themselves. Then slowly other children began to arrive. Many of them had new bikes, scooters and rollerblades.

Finally it was time to go back to the B&B and wash and get ready for lunch. As Megan, Sam and mum made their way across the hotel reception area towards the lift, they didn't spot two people sitting in the large sofa in the corner.

'It's about time,' said a familiar voice.

Megan looked round and to her great surprise there was Johnnie sitting next to his mum on the large green sofa. Between them, in the middle of the sofa, were two Christmas presents wrapped in sparkling silver wrapping paper.

'What are you doing here?' asked Megan, not exactly sure if she was angry or not.

'Look, I found out where you live by accident,' said Johnnie, not wanting to upset Megan. 'I had to go to the dentist, just across the road and I saw you come in here with your mum. So I came and asked if you lived here and they said that you did.'

'Oh,' said Megan unable to meet Johnnie's gaze.

'Look, my dad's cheque finally arrived. So if it's okay with your mum, my family got these presents for you and Sam,' continued Johnnie, pointing to the gifts on the sofa.

At this point, Johnnie's mum introduced herself and explained things in more detail. Finally, she revealed that Johnnie had wanted nothing for Christmas – except a new pair of trainers –

if Johnnie's mum and dad got these presents for Megan and Sam. Megan felt her eyes fill with tears.

'Don't worry,' said Johnnie's mum as she ruffled Megan's hair. 'He got his mountain bike as well.'

'Thank you so much,' said Megan's mum. 'I really don't know what to say.'

'There's no need to say anything. Now we'll leave you to open the presents and have your lunch,' said Johnnie's mum.

Megan was speechless. Then, before she realized what she was doing, she reached out and hugged Johnnie. Johnnie was clearly astonished.
'Listen, Meg. I want you to promise me something,' said Johnnie anxiously.
'What?' said Megan.

'Promise me that you won't tell my mates that you hugged me,' said Johnnie quite seriously.

'Okay,' said Megan smiling. 'I won't tell them.'

And with that Johnnie and his mum said goodbye and walked out of the hotel.

Megan picked up the sparkling packages and carried them towards the lift. Mum smiled at her and she smiled back.

'I bet you can't wait to open your present,' said mum.

Megan nodded. But she already knew what was inside.

You might not think that one person or a small group of people can do that much to change the world. But you'd be surprised what people with a great deal of determination can do!

MOTHER TERESA
1910–1997

Mother Teresa was born in Skopje, Macedonia. Her original name was Agnes Gonxha Bojaxhiu. At the age of 12, she decided that she wanted to devote her life to helping the poor. When she was 18 years old she travelled to Ireland to join a religious order of nuns and train to be a missionary.

Teresa was sent to work in India. To begin with, from 1929 to 1948, Teresa taught at a High School in Calcutta. But each day, as she witnessed the suffering and poverty in the streets, she became more and more determined to do something to help. Without any funds, she started an open-air school for homeless children.

On 7 October 1950, Mother Teresa received permission to start her own order called The Missionaries of Charity. Mother Teresa and her fellow missionaries devoted themselves to caring for people who nobody else was prepared to look after. Today over 1000 missionaries carry on her work in India.

EGLANTYNE JEBB
1876–1928

At the end of the First World War, the Allies (much of Europe and America) continued to blockade Germany and Austria to force them to accept peace. This meant that they couldn't receive food, cloth and medical supplies. Before long, children in the cities of Berlin and Vienna were starving.

A brave group of women in Britain spoke out against what was happening in Germany and Austria. They said that instead of punishing those responsible for war, the Allies' actions were killing innocent children.

Eglantyne Jebb, with the help of her sister Dorothy, led the campaign. They began by distributing leaflets and writing letters. Then they organized a meeting in London's Albert Hall in 1919. At this meeting the Save the Children organization was established. Its aim was to send food to starving children in Austria, Germany and other parts of Europe. Within a few years, Save the Children was helping all over the world, as it still does today.

BIG FAMILY

In ancient Rome all kinds of relatives lived together in the same house. Not only grandparents but great grandparents too. And then there were first cousins, second cousins, uncles and aunts. Just imagine all those relatives telling you what to do!

WELCOME

Ancient Greeks thought that their children were not fully mature until they were 30 years old! When a child was born, the father carried it, in a ritual dance, around the household. The family decorated the doorway of their home with a wreath of olives (for a boy) or a wreath of wool (for a girl).

PEOPLE'S PLANET

In 1999, the number of people on Earth reached 6 billion. By 2050, the world population is expected to be more than 9 billion people. Much of this growth will be in the poorest parts of the world.

⭐ HATS OFF
Until the eighteenth century in Britain, boys were expected to take off their hats in their parent's presence, and girls were expected to kneel before their mother.

⭐ CHILD LABOUR
If you had been a child in Medieval times you would have had lots of domestic chores to do, including looking after younger brothers and sisters, doing housework or helping in the fields. However, rich boys went to school and some girls boarded in noble households to study and learn good manners.

⭐ YOUNG ADULT
In Medieval Britain, you became an adult when you were 12 years old, with adult responsibilities.

⭐ GREEDY RICH
The richest fifth of the world consumes 45 per cent of meat and fish, 58 per cent of all energy and 84 per cent of all paper. It also owns 74 per cent of all telephone lines and 84 per cent of all vehicles.

Viking Superwife

Viking girls married between the ages of 12 and 16. Their parents or guardians chose their husbands. From the moment they married, they were in charge of the home. Their duties included cooking, weaving, looking after the farm animals, making butter and cheese, making sure food lasted through the winter months and, of course, preparing meals.

Off You Go!

In the seventeenth century Britain, poor and homeless children were shipped off to America where they were put to work as servants.

True Saying

A famous ancient Greek called Aristotle said that 'without friends no one would choose to live, though he had all other goods'.

THINGS TO DO

Dear Reader

Here are some things to do to make you think about how you interact with people. Perhaps you could ask a friend to join in with you.

1 Make a list of the names of everyone you met on one particular day. Think about how you handled these encounters. Could you, or would you, do things differently next time?

2 Write a letter to the adult members of your family and thank them for all the things they do for you.

3 Offer to help a little bit more with various chores at home.

4 Become a friend to a new pupil at school. Help them with things they feel unsure of. Invite them to play with you and your friends. Or befriend a younger child at school – someone who could use a special friend to look out for them.

5 Write a poem about friendship and what you think it means to be a friend.

6 Become a pen pal to a child in a poor country.

7 Adopt a charity that you care about and raise money for it.

8 Offer to help to look after the school pets.

9 If you haven't given much thought to where your food comes from, it's time to start. For example, you could choose to research tea – try to find out what is involved in growing and harvesting the tea plant. Find out what the workers have to do, how many hours they have to work, how much they get paid, and so on. Compare their work day to your parent's or guardian's.

10 Create a project on the life of a child in a poor country. Find out as much as you can about what their daily life is like. Try to find out what they eat, what clothes they wear, what their home is like, if they go to school, how many brothers and sisters they have and what games they like to play.

ASKING FOR HELP

Here are the contact details for organizations that offer help, advice and information to young people.

www.bullying.co.uk
Gives good advice to parents and children on how to cope with bullying.

www.atschool.co.uk
Information and activities related to a wide range of school topics and topics of general interest.

www.youthinformation.com
Information on a wide range of subjects such as health, the environment, school topics, justice and equality.

www.ncb.org.uk
National Children's Bureau provides information about social, political and environmental issues and encourages young people to get involved.

www.nchafc.org.uk
NCH Action for Children offers help to children and families affected by poverty, neglect or abuse.

www.savethechildren.org.uk
The UK's leading international children's charity; dedicated to creating a better future for children worldwide.

www.princes-trust.org.uk
The Prince's Trust aims to provide young people with a guiding and helping hand so that they can fulfil their true potential.

Childline UK 0800 1111
Free helpline for children in trouble or in danger
24 hours, 7 days a week.

NSPCC
0800 800 500
A 24-hour helpline for children in need of help.

NATIONAL CHILDREN'S BUREAU
020 7843 6000
Lots of advice on a wide range of topics.

BELIEF Something that a person thinks is true or real.

BULLY A person who teases, threatens or hurts someone.

CHARITY An organization dedicated to helping a particular cause.

CO-OPERATION Working together, assisting and helping.

DONATE To give money, things or your time.

EXPERIENCE Knowledge gained by doing and seeing things.

EXPLOIT To take advantage of a person or a situation.

GLOBAL Something to do with the whole world.

GUIDE To show the way.

POVERTY The condition of being poor.

RELATE To connect or understand.

RESPECT To honour someone.

RESPONSIBILITY To feel a sense of duty and trust.

INJUSTICE Something that is unfair.

INTERACT To act or be involved with others.

LOYALTY To be faithful and true to someone.

MALNOURISHED When someone does not have a balanced, healthy diet.

POOR To have nothing or very little.

SHARE To divide or give so that everyone is included.

TRUST To believe in something or someone.

VIEW A way of looking at something.

47

INDEX